The

Wicca
Bible

The
Wicca
Bible

THE DEFINITIVE GUIDE
TO MAGIC AND THE CRAFT

Ann-Marie Gallagher

Bounty
BOOKS

First published in Great Britain in 2005
by Godsfield Press, a division of
Octopus Publishing Group Ltd
Revised edition published in 2009

This edition published in 2011 by Bounty Books
a division of Octopus Publishing Group Ltd
Endeavour House, 189 Shaftesbury Avenue
London WC2H 8JY
www.octopusbooks.co.uk

An Hachette UK Company
www.hachette.co.uk

ISBN: 978-0-75372-132-2

A CIP catalogue record for this book is available
from the British Library

Printed and bound in China

Contents

Introduction

Wicca is the religion and practice of witches, or 'the Wise', as we are sometimes known. It has been described as the fastest-growing religion in the West, though nobody really knows how many Wiccans there are in the world. Judging by the number of internet sites and formal groups cropping up around the globe, particularly in Britain, continental Europe and the USA, it is clear that the growth of the Wiccan movement is quite phenomenal.

Perhaps this is not all that surprising. Over the last few decades, public interest in the environment, in alternative healing therapies, self-development, holistic food and medicine, social justice and, significantly, in 'alternative' spiritualities and magic has developed tremendously. Wicca explores many of these concerns within an inclusive spiritual path that honours the diversity and divinity of nature and advises its followers to 'harm none'. If you read carefully through the different sections of this book, participate in the activities it guides

Wicca is a nature religion. Wiccans see the divine in nature, both within us and around us.

you through and learn more about practising Wicca, you will begin to understand exactly why Wicca, sometimes called 'the Craft', has grown in popularity and why, in the twenty-first century, people are declaring themselves 'Wicce' or 'Witches'.

Because Wicca is a religion that does not have a doctrine or a set central priesthood, sacred texts or sets of rules, the responsibility for learning and growing within the chosen spiritual path is placed upon the individual. Even though there are some established traditions within the Wiccan community, many have grown out of exploration and continue to evolve as Wiccans learn which practices and points of understanding are essential, and which are more flexible.

Practising spirituality outside the limiting strictures of a set 'organized' religion can be a very liberating experience, but it can also be extraordinarily demanding on the individual, requiring considerable resourcefulness. Some novices will be lucky enough to have friends or family who are Wiccan, and thus have good sources of advice only a phonecall away. The majority of us, though, start out with an interest that we want to explore privately before joining a group or sounding out others for counsel.

The main purpose of this book is to provide a detailed resource of information – and inspiration – both for those who are encountering Wicca for the first time and for those who are already treading that path. All the information and guidance you need on the key aspects of Wicca as a philosophy, a spiritual path and a magical tradition are explored. Knowledge of these key aspects will help direct you through the exciting territory that is Wiccan spirituality and practice, and help you develop your own understanding and sense of the spiritual on your travels.

Wiccans recognize the value of continuing to develop our understanding and practices; just as the world constantly changes around us, so we, too, must acknowledge the need to grow and extend our knowledge and skills. There is scope within the book for those who already have some knowledge of the ways of the Wise to develop that further, or to revisit their understanding of different aspects of Wicca.

Welcome, then, to Wicca as it is practised by the Wise, with its regional variations and in its many diverse flavours all over the globe. Welcome also to a tradition that casts a look over its shoulder into the past to find a spiritual affinity with our ancestors, and looks forward to the future for new ways of living with each other, with the rhythms of the Earth and nature. And if you are setting your foot on the path of the Wise, then as the Wicce say, Blessed Be.

The chalice is a symbol of healing, communion and initiation.

Wicca works with the rhythms and tides of nature.

how to use the book

For the beginner, the best and most effective way to use this book when reading it for the first time is to work through it in order, trying the various exercises as you proceed. It is also best, if you are new to Wicca, to read through What is Wicca? (see pages 14–47), which will give you a good foundation for what follows.

Each section has an introductory segment with background and guidance to the information and exercises that follow. It is important to read the introductions carefully as they often define and explain terminology and provide information vital to the practical work in the sections. For example, the introduction to Visualization (see pages 132–39) offers a beginner's guide to visualization, including practical guidance on how to prepare physically and how to create the sacred space in which to work. Ignoring this advice may adversely affect your progress through the exercises and lead to frustration. In particular, if you are tempted to dip into the spells in Magic (see pages 242–77), it is vital that you read the introduction that explains the principles, laws and ethics to which practising magicians adhere.

For the more experienced, it is still a good idea to read through What is Wicca? (see pages 14–47) so that you are clear about the basis on which this book is written. Beyond that, your experience will enable you to dip in and out of the text at will for information, ideas and inspiration for your solo or coven work. However, remember to read the introduction to any section you intend to dip into as this will remind you of

Preparation is important. This witch censes the sacred space prior to ritual.

Traditionally, handfasting lasts for a year and a day.

the basic disciplines and reasoning behind the way the section is presented. If you are a teacher, you may find good resource material on the passage of the Wiccan year and its eight Sabbats (see pages 48–73) as well as some suggested activities for attuning to the five sacred Elements (see pages 74–89).

The beginner and experienced practitioner alike will find a wealth of information within Paths and traditions (see pages 90–101) which is based on experience of and research into Wiccan beliefs and practices. You will find explanations or reminders of the importance to witches of the circle and sacred space, as well as directions on how to create that space. Similarly, you will be the planet for our survival. But what does it mean to be an animal that has a capacity for abstract thought and language, is aware of its individual consciousness and its own search for spiritual meaning?

Such questions are the first step along the way to spiritual discovery, but they can only be answered through the experience of the journey itself. In Wicca, it is this journey itself that is the meaning. This is implied by the child's natural

The spiritual journey begins with questions about our place in the cosmos.

tendency to start at the beginning and work outwards in steps until we reach 'the Universe'. Seeing nature as a continuum, rather than something that stops outside our front doors, is something that we have to relearn.

RHYTHMS OF THE WORLD

In Wicca, newcomers are encouraged to learn a little basic physics regarding the place of the Earth in the solar system and the physical interaction of the Sun and the Moon with the Earth's seasons and tides in order to better understand the natural rhythms with which we work.

MARKERS OF THE SACRED CYCLE

The Earth's tilt is the basis of the seasons — the inclination of its axis means that at times we are closer to the Sun and as the temperature and the weather change on a cyclical basis, so the vegetation and life on the planet respond. In the Wiccan year, there are four solar festivals. These are markers of astronomical events; the shortest and longest days at the winter and summer solstices and the two days of perfect balance between the hours of daylight and darkness at the spring and autumn equinoxes. In the northern hemisphere the shortest day at the winter solstice usually falls on 21 or 22 December, the longest day at the summer solstice on 21 or 22 June, the spring equinox on 21 or 22 March and the autumn equinox on 21 or 22 September. In the southern hemisphere the solstices and the equinoxes are reversed. These events are seen as four struts on the wheel of the year, important markers of the sacred cycle.

THE LUNAR CYCLE

The Moon, our closest celestial neighbour, produces the tides on the waters of Earth and influences the reproductive cycles of some animals. The full cycle of the Moon through its phases from new (or dark) Moon, first quarter, half, full, last quarter and back to new or dark again is 29.5 days. Although the word 'month' is taken from the word 'Moon', our calendar does not faithfully follow lunar cycles, of which there are thirteen rather than twelve in a year.

One of the first things that people learn about the Craft is the importance to witches of the lunar cycles for the timing of spells and rituals. Similarly, some activities and spells are timed with the seasons, set in relation to the Earth's dance around the Sun.

The wonder of the cyclical relationships of Earth, Sun, Moon and stars inspires and moves us closer to knowledge of ourselves and our place in the cosmos. In Wicca we try to carry out our research on the physical, experience it for ourselves and express it poetically.

The lunar cycle is particularly important to witches.

Life cycles

The sense of change in the biological and social events of our own lives is also celebrated in Wicca. Accordingly, witches celebrate a number of aspects of the human life cycle as sacred and special.

In common with others, witches celebrate the three common rites of passage – birth, marriage and death – with naming ceremonies, marriage or 'handfasting' ceremonies and funeral rites. These are the most commonly recognized life-cycle events in Western societies. Other aspects of our biological and social life cycles that are not as commonly celebrated, however, are highly valued in Wicca.

Witches celebrate many aspects of change in our life cycles.

A birth is regarded as a blessing, and childhood, a time when we interact with the world in simple, immediate terms, is seen as particularly sacred. But we also value the transition from childhood to puberty, adolescence and adulthood, as part of the constant change that marks our lives. In most Western societies, the biological changes from girlhood to womanhood, from boyhood to manhood, are not marked or celebrated. Indeed, the whole issue of menstruation, let alone the menarche (first menstrual period) is generally a secretive process, where silence rather than celebration rules. In Wicca, we celebrate a young woman's first moon-blood, because we see this as a sacred event. Sometimes we celebrate the deepening of a young man's voice, so that he can join the world of men in a

Brighid. Imbolc marks the quickening of the Earth, the first thaws after winter, the birth of the lambs and the first signs that spring is coming. Continuing around the wheel, between Ostara and Litha, is Beltane (pronounced either bell-tayne or bile-tin), meaning 'bright fire'. Beltane is celebrated when the first May-blossom blooms or on the first Full Moon thereafter (see dates for both hemispheres in the box on page 50). Beltane celebrates the greening of the Earth and all aspects of fertility in vegetation, birds and animals, and is associated with the Green Man, a spirit or god of nature.

Between Litha and Modron comes Lughnasadh (pronounced loo-na-sah) or Lammas, celebrated when the first corn sheaf is cut or the first Full Moon after that (see dates for both hemispheres in the box on page 50). Lughnasadh celebrates the cereal harvest and the gathering in of blessings and honours the spirit of plenty that brings the corn to ripeness. Finally, between Modron and Yule is the Sabbat known as Samhain (pronounced sow-ain) meaning 'first frost'. As its name suggests, this is sometimes celebrated when the first frosts come, or on the first Full Moon thereafter (see dates for both hemispheres in the box on page 50). This is the Feast of the Ancestors, the Day of the Dead and also the old Celtic New Year, where we leave the warmer days behind and go down into the darkness that will lead us back to Yule.

It is an old tradition, for the Celtic fire festivals at least, that the festival begins at sundown the day before and ends on the following sundown. This means that if you celebrate Beltane on 1 May, the festival actually begins at sundown on 30 April.

These, then, are the eight great Wiccan Sabbats, the radials of the year's wheel. Exploring the customs and the meanings of the various festivals will help you to understand more about pagan spirituality. Experiencing for yourself the way that witches work with Gaia's many tides and seasons will also help you to attune to the spirit of nature and understand better the changes and shifts that occur in your own life.

SECRET RITES

Imbolc is very much a women's festival, and, traditionally, for the first part of the celebration, women practise their own rites which are never spoken of outside the circle or when men are present. The men, of course, have their own mysteries to practise while they wait to be invited into the circle as honoured guests. They bring gifts for Brighid, which are laid at the feet of a *bridiog* — an effigy of the goddess which is dressed and decorated by the women and placed in a basket. Throughout the ritual, celebrants may approach the *bridiog* to whisper to her their secrets and wishes.

Brighid is a goddess of healing, inspiration of poets and patron of blacksmiths and metalworkers. She is the fire in the head of poets and the fire in the belly of those who act upon their ideas — a goddess of inspiration and action. As patron of metalworkers, she is the key to turning raw materials into useful and beautiful things — a goddess of transformation. At Imbolc, a time of renewal, we celebrate changes around and within us, and renew our commitment to making the world a better place. We honour the spark of divine creativity within us and raise healing energy.

The Chalice Well at Chalice Well Garden in Glastonbury, England.

Ostara – the vernal equinox

Ostara marks the vernal (meaning youthful) equinox – a time of balance between daylight and darkness, the point before day is longer than night. It falls in the Christian season of Lent in the northern hemisphere (see the box on page 50 for dates in the southern hemisphere), which itself comes from an Anglo-Saxon word, referring to the 'lengthening' of the days.

It is also a celebration of growth and derives its name from a German goddess whose totem was the hare. The saying 'Mad as a March hare' comes from observations of their mating behaviour at this time of year, as they appear to 'box' and leap about in the fields. In fact, hares are no more crazy in their behaviour in March than at any other time; it is just that the grass is still short enough for their antics to be visible! The hare is seen as prolifically fertile and many Moon goddesses linked with women's reproductive cycles share it as a totem of earthy

The hare is sacred to the goddess of the Moon.

within us. It is important, therefore, to work towards building a relationship with Air at a physical as well as a symbolic level.

The symbolic functions of Air are concerned with reason, learning, intellectual knowledge, communication, the law, movement, expedition and language. The physical gifts of Air are breath, the wind, sound, scent and memory. Collect symbols that encapsulate the element of Air and work with Air through your breath-work, meditating on your chosen symbols and conscious contact with Air in the natural world.

Ritual staffs and wands symbolize Air.

RITUAL WELCOME TO AIR

[Officer for Air]: *In the east, the element of Air; communication, reason and memory, our first breath and our last, you are honoured in this circle. Be present at our rites and bring to this circle your gifts of clarity, teaching, learning and understanding.*

[Officer lights a yellow candle in the east]: *Hail and welcome!*

[All]: *Hail and welcome!*

fire
INSPIRATION, PASSION AND COURAGE

In ritual space, the Fire quarter is often decorated in red, with candles, lamps, carved dragons or salamanders, flowers and associated herbs, spices and gums such as frankincense, cinnamon, cactus or coriander, and athames (witches' knives) or swords. Symbols or images of deities associated with Fire may be included: Brighid, Celtic fire goddess or Belenos, god of the Sun. We burn lamps and candles in the south of our circles as physical representations

Blades often represent Fire.

working with fire

1 Walk through a park or town on a sunny day. Become conscious of the warmth of the Sun on your face, and the light that penetrates your closed eyelids.

2 How are the people, animals or plants around you affected by the light and heat of the Sun?

3 Another form of Fire is electricity. In mild weather, if you are at home alone, turn off all but strictly essential sources of electricity for one evening. Spend the evening in candlelight, without TV or music. If you can, light a bonfire outside.

4 How does the lack of electricity affect your activities? What do you experience with the different forms of fire you are using to create light and heat?

RITUAL WELCOME TO FIRE

[Officer for Fire]: *In the south, the element of Fire; inspiration, passion and courage, the spark that ignited our existence, you are honoured in this circle. Be present at our rites and bring to this circle your gifts of willpower, daring and creativity.*

[Officer lights a red candle in the south]: *Hail and welcome!*

[All]: *Hail and welcome!*

Lamps symbolize light as a gift of Fire.

of Fire. In order to summon our inner Fire, we need to connect with and understand its function in the physical Universe as well as within Wiccan symbolism. This requires a little time set aside to consider the element in all its aspects and to experience its material function in our own lives.

The symbolic functions of Fire are inspiration, willpower, courage, activity and energy, and empowerment. The physical gifts of Fire are flame, combustion, electricity, warmth and light, body-heat and the rays of the Sun. Assemble some symbols that represent Fire and continue working with it through your conscious contact with its various forms in everyday life, and by meditating on your chosen symbols.

Water
INTUITION, DREAMS AND EMOTIONS

In our rituals, the Water quarter is often decorated in blue, with glass pebbles, depictions of sea-creatures, 'watery' herbs and flowers such as roses, hyacinths, myrtle and lovage, and a chalice. We may add symbols or images of Water-associated deities, such as Rhiannon, Welsh goddess of rebirth, or Yemana, Santeria goddess of the sea. Working with the element of Water involves having direct knowledge of the vital purpose it serves in our physical environment as well as understanding its symbolic nature and meaning. In order to 'connect' with Water, set aside time to find out more about it and experience for yourself its physical impact on our daily lives.

WORKING WITH WATER

1 Go to a beach or shore of a tidal sea, river or lake, and walk along the edge of the water at low tide. Walk with your eyes cast down towards the ground.

2 What do you see? How has the water affected its form? Observe the humans on the shore. What are they doing? Where are they looking? What attracts humans to watersides?

3 Research your local tides in the library or on the internet.

4 Set aside time to meditate; close your eyes and place the index finger of your left hand on the bone on the inside of your right wrist on your pulse. How does it feel to know that you carry rivers, streams and tributaries inside you? What function do streams and rivers serve on our planet?

about other people's choices and recognize, being truly wise, the importance of diversity rather than conformity.

The following descriptions of the different paths and various affinities of groups and solo workers are indicative rather than definitive. If you want to learn more about a particular tradition, there is a plethora of resources in libraries, bookshops and on the internet to explore further. I have included a brief reference to groups that are non-Wiccan, mainly because witches often find themselves rubbing shoulders with them. If you should find that your own practices cross over into different traditions, don't worry; most witches come under the 'eclectic' grouping!

Witchcraft is a diverse path with many traditions.

Different paths

The roots of modern Wicca are found all over Europe and the near East, in the spiritual focus of our ancestors and in strands of paganism that have withstood the buffeting of time by disguising themselves as folklore and country wisdom. The story of modern Wicca's awakening, however, is far more recent and began in England in 1951 with the repeal of the 1736 Witchcraft Act, subsequently replaced by the Fraudulent Mediums Act. The impetus for its

The roots of Wicca are both recent and ancient.

repeal was its employment in the prosecution in 1944 of a spiritualist medium Helen Duncan, who attracted the attention of the naval authorities by revealing to members of the public the sinking of ships whose details had not yet been publicly released. The fact that the Act was still on the statute books incensed a number of public figures, who were concerned that its existence was a slur on the reputation of British law, and consequently it was repealed.

The Act's repeal effectively legalized witchcraft in England and enabled the publication of works describing the practices of covens.

FOUNDER OF MODERN WICCA

Gerald Gardner, recognized as the founder of modern Wicca, had already published in 1949 a fictional work titled *High Magic's Aid*. However, with the repeal of the Witchcraft Act and the death of his high priestess Old Dorothy Clutterbuck in that same year, he was free to write a non-fictional account of Wicca: *Witchcraft Today*, published in 1954. Although much of Gardner's work was based on the practices of covens operating in the early twentieth century and borrowed heavily from ancient esoteric documentation, he was also influenced by the work of some of his contemporaries, and included some flourishes of his own.

Debates about Gardner's *Book of Shadows* – the recorded litany, customs, spells and rituals of a witch – continue. Most people now credit his high priestess Doreen Valiente with the emphasis given to the Goddess. She is also the author of the *Mother Charge*, the words of the Goddess to her people, with which many Wiccan groups still open their Esbats or Full Moon celebrations. However, Gardner's contribution was seminal to the development of modern Wicca and since its early foundation it has grown to encompass a whole range of approaches and traditions.

The following are examples of some of the key expressions of the many different styles and flavours of Wicca, but remember that a paragraph cannot possibly encapsulate the meaning of a tradition which has its own influences, history and customs. If you want to learn more, you will need to do some research or better still, talk to a practising member of that tradition to learn more about it.

GARDNERIAN WICCA

Named for Gerald Gardner, this tradition enfolds elements of ancient traditions and, because of its local origins, the folklore and customs of English paganism. It uses the basic pattern of a ritual circle, and elemental quarters for Air, Fire, Earth and Water, though the colour symbolism differs from most other Wiccan traditions in that the colour for Air is blue, for Earth, brown or black and for Water, green.

Gardnerians tend not to emphasize the element of Spirit.

All paths of Wicca have a nature-orientation.

Gardnerian Wicca venerates the Horned God of the Greenwood and the Goddess of Nature. Generally, Gardnerian Wicca is celebrated while 'sky-clad' – naked. A high priest and high priestess lead each coven, with emphasis on the leadership of the high priestess. The Gardnerian system marks spiritual progress by a series of initiatory rites and is based on gender bi-polarity, which means that all things are divided into masculine/feminine opposites.

ALEXANDRIAN WICCA

This form of Wicca developed out of the Gardnerian system in the 1960s and is named for Alex Sanders, who with his partner Maxine developed a tradition that incorporated elements of Judaeo-Christian sources, as well as aspects of the Greek and Egyptian mysteries and Celtic traditions.

Alexandrians honour the triple Goddess in all her aspects (maiden, mother and crone) and dual God (dark and light) – though some practitioners are also eclectic in their approach to deities. Alexandrian Wicca uses the basic framework set down by Gardnerian Wicca, but honours five sacred elements and uses the now widely recognized colour symbolism set out on pages 78.

SAXON WICCA

Saex-Wicca was formulated by Raymond Buckland in the early 1970s. He is also accredited with introducing Wicca to the USA. Saex-Wicca is based on the Gardnerian framework, but draws in aspects of English Saxon and Scots Pictish traditions.

HEDGEWITCHES AND SOLITARIES

The traditions outlined above are generally practised in groups, but in Wicca there are many witches who practise on their own. The accurate title of this group is 'Solitaries', and they may practise any tradition of Wicca; what sets them apart is that they work alone. Solo workers are sometimes called 'Hedgewitches', though strictly speaking Hedgewitchery is the work of a Wise-Woman or Cunning-Man serving a community, knowledgeable in the ways of nature, herbal magic and traditional healing. The niceties of distinction are not always observed, however, and some city witches are keen to use the term to emphasize the origins of their spiritual path.

HEREDITARY

In Wicca, an Hereditary is a witch who has inherited Craft knowledge through their own family, or initiation into an hereditary group. Since the practices of such groups will differ according to what has been passed on to them, it is almost impossible to pinpoint what any particular Hereditary practises.

RADICAL FAERY/DIANIC WICCA/RECLAIMING TRADITION

In theory there is no reason why Wicca should not be socially inclusive, but unfortunately some individuals or groups use, for example, gender bi-polarity to justify their own homophobia or sexism. Consequently, some witches have worked to create positive spiritual space for women, bisexuals, lesbians and gay men. The Radical Faery tradition was created by and for gay men, and in some groups there is an emphasis on the God Dionysus.

Most Dianic groups are either exclusively lesbian or female, and as their name suggests, the Goddess Diana is their chief patron. The Reclaiming Tradition, influenced by the work of Starhawk and Macha M Nightmare, is inclusive, politically active and outspoken on issues of all forms of social discrimination. They operate on a non-hierarchical basis, organize public rituals and camps, and are the 'ecstatics' of the US movement, using trance and shamanistic methods in their practices.

ECLECTICISM

All witches are, to an extent, eclectic, but Eclectics are those who do not align themselves with any particular tradition and instead select, borrow, appropriate and redefine to suit their purpose, elements of other traditions. All done respectfully, of course!

Nephthys Goddess of magic and secret knowledge. Nephthys is a beloved sister of Isis and contemporary witches call on her to empower them with arcane knowledge and the skills with which to activate our innate magical powers. She is a goddess of sisterhood, darkness, childbirth and nursing. She is also a goddess of secrecy. Her magician status makes her particularly popular with witches.
Origins: Egypt.
Symbols and associations: Kite (bird).

Nut Goddess of the night sky. Nut is a primal deity whose whole body forms the vault of the heavens. She is sometimes depicted as arching over the Earth, her body the blue of the sky and fire of the stars. A basic creation deity.
Origins: Egypt.
Symbols and associations: Astronomy, the night sky, stars.

Osiris God of regeneration. Osiris is credited with bringing all the trappings of civilization to Egypt, as well as being a deity of corn and wine, crafts and religion. Like his son Horus, he is a god of the rising and the setting Sun, and is associated with regeneration because he was cut to pieces by Set before being reassembled by his sister/lover Isis, with whom he conceived their falcon-headed son (see Isis and Horus above). Nowadays, Osiris retains many of his original aspects as god of life, death and regeneration.
Origins: Egypt.
Symbols and associations: Corn, vine leaves.

Sehkmet Lion-headed goddess. Destroyer of disease and disposer of unwanted things, Sekhmet is a solar deity, closely associated with Bast. She is independent and fiery, and is called upon when there is heavy magical work to be done!
Origins: Egypt.
Symbols and associations: Lion-heads, sun discs.

Set God of the waning Moon, thunder and storms. He is an impatient, uncontrollable life-force, and in ancient times represented drought and destruction. Nowadays, his function is similar to that of Sekhmet, the necessary cutting away of surplus.

Origins: Egypt.

Symbols and associations: Waning Moon, lightning fork.

Thoth God of magic, wisdom, medicine, astronomy and writing, but especially of music. Said to have brought all magic and wisdom into being with the power of sound; Thoth is a great favourite with contemporary magicians who use incantation, drumming and song to invoke him. God of great knowledge.

Origins: Egypt.

Symbols and associations: Crescent Moon, the Eye of Ra (the Sun).

CELTIC AND NORTHERN EUROPEAN DEITIES

Angus/Oengus Celtic god of love and youth. Unusually a male representation of love and beauty. His music draws lovers of music and beauty to him. His kisses were said to turn into singing birds.

Origins: Ireland/Scotland.

Symbols and associations: Harp, songbirds.

Arhianrhod Goddess of 'the Silver Wheel', the Moon and the stars. In Welsh mythology, the constellation *Corona Borealis* is known as 'Caer Arhianrhod', the tower or castle of Arhianrhod. Connected with spinning and weaving, Arhianrhod is a goddess of connections, particularly those between birth, death and regeneration. She is a wisdom figure who keeps the knowledge of the past, the present and the future in her crystal tower. She represents deep soul knowledge, intuition and the mysteries of the life cycle.

Origin: Wales.
Symbols and associations: Spinning wheel, webs, the Full Moon, stars.

Belenos/Bel The Celtic Sun god dubbed 'the British Apollo' by the Romans. Deity of light, health and healing, Belenos was thought – in some parts of northern Europe – to drive a chariot carrying the Sun's disc. In his healing aspect, he is associated with healing waters, wells and springs. The prefix 'Bel' means shining and was often linked with solar and aquatic deities, such as the Romano-British goddess 'Belisama' (shining one), so it is unsurprising that his image is found carved into the first-century BCE temple at Aqua Sulis, a natural spa in Bath, England. His name is given to the May festival of 'Beltane', which means literally 'the fire of the God Bel', and part of the seasonal festival celebrating the rise of the Sun. His victory over the hours of darkness is celebrated at Litha, the summer solstice, and his imminent fall is marked by the sending of fiery wheels down hillsides at that time of year.
Origins: Northern Europe, Britain.
Symbols and associations: Wheel, sunburst, head with penumbra or halo.

Bel/Beli/Sol The female aspect of Bel/Belenos (see above), Bel or Beli is celebrated as a goddess in feminist and goddess-centred Wicca, and has many of the aspects attributed to her male counterpart. However, Bel is also seen as the inner, as well as the outer, physical Sun, and a link between the healing, regenerative power of the Sun and the nurturing, restorative power of the soul.
Origins: Northern Europe, Britain.
Symbols and associations: Tidal rivers, the wheel, sunbursts, serpentine hair, May Day morning dew.

Brighid/Bridie/Brigit Celtic fire goddess associated with healing, poetry and metalwork. The triple goddess Brighid has close connections with the Sun and

her fire aspect is seen as the warming breath that warms the Earth to end winter and bring the thaw and the first snowdrops. Brighid is midwife to the spring, and is a protector of women, children and newborn animals, particularly sheep and cattle. Many healing shrines, wells and springs in England and Ireland are named for her. She is associated with serpents – ancient symbol of the healing powers of the Earth Goddess – and her festival is at Imbolc (or Oimelc), a time associated with the birth of lambs. Today Brighid is a goddess of independence, integrity and energy, often depicted in her threefold aspect with fiery red hair.
Origins: Ireland, Scotland, Isle of Man, England.
Symbols and associations: *Fire, wells, healing cauldron, serpents, anvil and hammer, dandelion, snowdrops, amethysts, white candles.*

Bloddueth Maiden goddess of springtime and flowers. A 'Green Woman' for the late spring, Bloddueth in Welsh legends is built from flowers by a magician to provide a wife for the divine hero, Llew Llaw Gyffes, son of Arhianrhod. In this legend, Bloddueth is portrayed as deceitful and is turned into an owl as punishment. Present-day pagans interpret this story slightly differently, seeing Bloddueth's dual nature as spirit of Sun and Moon, as an aspect of the goddess involved in the initiation of the hero. Further, goddess-centred pagans

Herne leading the Wild Hunt in Richmond Park, England.

122

ASIAN, AFRICAN AND MIDDLE EASTERN DEITIES

Astarte/Ishtar Goddess of love and sexuality, female allurement and primal creatrix. Associated with the stars, Moon and Sun as well as the Earth, she is also an ancient mother goddess archetype, linking sexuality and reproduction, sensuality and spirituality. A goddess of dance and beauty, like Aphrodite associated with the planet Venus.

Origins: Asia.

Symbols and associations: Serpents, stars, the Milky Way.

Innanna Goddess of the heavens and the Underworld, Innanna is an independent and spirited figure. She is a Moon goddess as well as an Earth deity. Her adventures in the Underworld are similar to those of many gods and goddesses who undergo sacrifice in order to gain wisdom and knowledge (see Odin page 128). She also has links with goddesses who venture into the Underworld, such as Persephone (see pages 114–15) and Freya (see pages 126–27), causing the vegetation on Earth to die, restoring it on her return, in the myth of the seasonal cycle. She is celebrated as a mistress of life and death, a wise woman and a trickster.

Origins: Ancient Sumer, Asia.

Symbols and associations: Seven stars in a circle, the Moon.

Kali Goddess of dance, female energy. Kali is part of the primal life-force. She dances the dance of

Kali represents part of the primal life-force.

'destruction' – that is to say the chaos out of which life is produced – and cuts away that which is not strictly necessary. In Wicca she is seen as a necessary aspect of creation, a positive way of channelling 'righteous' anger and putting energy to good use. She is a fierce protector and symbol of direct action in good causes.
Origins: India.
Symbols and associations: Fire and dance, the wheel of creation.

Lilith Owl-footed goddess of childbirth, integrity and resistance against tyranny. Lilith is the dark side of the Moon and represents aspects of femaleness often outlawed within patriarchy. She is a lunar deity who oversees women's monthly cycles, pregnancy and childbirth, and she protects newborns.
Origins: North Africa.
Symbols and associations: Owls, disc of the half-Moon.

Mithras God of light and resurrection. Although the cult of Mithras originated in Persia, he became particularly popular with Roman soldiers. Today, his rites are seen as a celebration of the redemptive and regenerative life force. Mithras is seen as a solar god and a god of vegetation. He links reason and intuition, and represents inner as well as outward illumination. Celebrated particularly at the solar festivals, his major festival is at the winter solstice, when he is reborn.
Origins: Persia, Asia, Europe.
Symbols and associations: Sunbursts.

Oya Goddess of storms, positive and protective action and defence. Oya is a fierce goddess, but good to have on your side if you are being threatened or bullied. She represents the basic instinct for self-protection and is not averse to bouncing back to wrongdoers the results of their own deeds.
Origins: Africa.
Symbols and associations: Copper shield, colour red.

how to prepare for visualization

1 Close your eyes. Take three deep breaths, breathing in calm and breathing out stress, anxieties and distracting thoughts.

2 The next seven breaths draw energy from the ground below you and the Earth below that, up through an imaginary column running through the centre of your body.

3 The first breath lights up the energy point or *chakra* at the base of your spine, which is a red light or flower. The second lights the sacral chakra (below the belly button), which is orange. The third breath activates the solar plexus chakra which is yellow; the fourth the heart chakra which is green; the fifth the throat chakra which is blue; and the sixth the third-eye chakra (forehead) which is violet.

4 The seventh breath opens the crown chakra of pure white light. Allow it to shower over you and connect back with the Earth energy upon which you are drawing.

5 Visualize a circle of white light all around you. This creates sacred space between the everyday world and the inner world to which you are journeying.

6 When your visualization is over and you have made notes, 'close down' the circle and the energy centres you have activated, leaving the base of spine chakra and crown chakra open just a little. Neglecting to 'close down' can leave you over-sensitized and vulnerable to other people's negative energies.

7 Eat and drink something to 'ground' yourself – this is important!

meeting your patron deity

This exercise is suitable for those wishing to encounter a patron deity. Try not to pre-empt a 'choice' of patron; let the right god or goddess choose you. You will be able to repeat this inner journey to visit your patron as much as you need to, to ask questions, receive knowledge, or spend time in their company. Aspects of this visualization are left open deliberately to allow your individual experience to fill in the gaps. Remember, the most significant details of your quest lie within you.

Details you encounter on your inner journeys are clues to guide you on your spiritual path.

VIZUALIZATION

Undertake preparations as detailed on pages 138–39.

1 Close your eyes, relax and enter the space behind your eyelids. Go into the darkness within and feel yourself dropping through the levels of consciousness. Imagine yourself in an elevator descending many levels, until it stops and the doors open. Step out into a candlelit passage. Proceed along the passage, noting the texture of the floor on your bare feet, the material of the walls and any decorations that are present. Note whether the passage is straight or bent.

2 You come to a doorway leading to a chamber. Is the doorway covered by a curtain, a door or a screen, or is it open? Pass through into the room beyond, paying attention to details of your surroundings. At the centre of the room is a tall plinth which you ascend by the means of steps. Approach whatever is on the plinth. The object holds a clue to your magical identity. Pick it up and inspect it, wear or eat it – whatever is appropriate to the object you find. When you are ready, step down from the plinth.

3 Notice a doorway leading out of the room – pass through this door into another passage. You may notice a flow of fresh air passing through the corridor as it leads you out into open terrain. What environment do you find yourself in? Is it day or night? What animals or plants, if any, surround you? Is there a preponderance of any one of the elements in this environment – lots of water or the presence of fire and heat? Spend some time here, as you may find further clues to your magical name. When ready, choose a spot to sit down and absorb the nature of this environment; wait for guidance to come.

4 You may be approached by a figure or an animal, or find your attention drawn to a tree, plant or some other aspect of this environment. This offers further clues to your magical name. You may even have this offered to you if a figure speaks with you. Whatever happens, remember to thank the figure, creature, tree, plant or element for their guidance.

5 When the surroundings have yielded all that they are prepared to in respect of your magical name, close your inward eyes and move back into the darkness. Mentally step into your 'elevator' and feel yourself ascending to the level of everyday consciousness. Slowly return to your surroundings, open your eyes ready to note the significant aspects of your inner journey. Follow the instructions on page 139 for 'closing down'.

Finding a magical name may take a little time and patience. You can combine this exercise with guidance offered on pages 216–17, or continue to meditate on it and take careful note of aspects that appear in your everyday life. Often such coincidences are the result of your enhanced attention and should be noted.

Clues to your magical name may be found around you in everyday life.

The temple of the Moon

In the mystical Qabalah (see pages 302–07), the sphere of the Moon is called 'Yesod' and is associated with the unconscious mind, with cycles of existence and with psychic and magical abilities. This ties in with the symbolism and experiences that witches associate with the Moon, and is a good starting point for those who wish to discover more about their spiritual direction. The following is a favourite in more traditional covens where newcomers are 'trained' by a high priest or priestess.

This inner journey helps new Wiccans move beyond the realm of the rational and into what I call 'Goddess-space'. This is the chaotic place-time of possibility and potential, the foundation of all creation and magic, which those who seek a magical life must experience. We need to be in touch with Moon energy to grow spiritually and extend our powers magically. This is a potent visualization, so it is advisable to leave at least three lunar cycle between visits.

The Moon is the ruler of dreams.

VISUALIZATION

Before undertaking preparations as detailed on pages 138–39, ensure that you are properly 'grounded', and have a familiar object close at hand that you can physically hold when you return from your inner journey. This will help to 'anchor' you in consensual reality when the visualization has ended.

1 Close your eyes and become aware of any intrusive thoughts. Mentally 'bat' them away as you prepare to enter the inner worlds.

2 As you enter the space within, become aware of the wash of waves in the distance. Allow this sound to become louder as you draw nearer to its source. Open your inner senses – feel the drag of breezes on your skin, the taste of salt, the sensation of dry sand under your feet. Open your inner vision to see that you are on a seashore. Take note of your surroundings. What colour is the sand, the sky? Walk to the water's edge until you find a craft. Step into

the boat and notice its colour, its details. Is anybody else in the boat? Do they speak to you? What do you notice as the boat moves out to sea? What do you hear?

3 When the boat lands, notice the details of its mooring place. This is a small island, joined to a vaster shore by a bridge. What does the bridge look like; what and who is on the other shore? You may hear voices or sounds that are familiar and strange, see faces you know and faces of strangers. Those who wish to speak to you will approach the far end of the bridge. You may face them from your side of the bridge, but you may not cross. If anybody wishes to speak with you, they will do so. You may speak with the dead; you are contacting that deep part of yourself that is their memory. When you have finished speaking, bid farewell and thank the guardian of the bridge for your time there. You may ask the guardian who they are and what their purpose is. Listen

carefully to the answers; you may wish to remember and note them down on your return.

4 Rest on your island. Think about your own life. What is your earliest memory? What have you learned during your lifetime so far? Who taught you these lessons? Are they alive or have they passed to the Summerlands? What part of them remains with you? When ready, return to the boat, and sail back to the shore from whence you came. How do you feel to leave that place? Is the journey back more difficult than the journey outwards? Who is with you on your journey?

5 As you disembark, thank whoever travels with you and concentrate on the feeling of firm ground beneath your feet. Physically pick up the object you have chosen as your 'anchor' and slowly return to your surroundings. If you are working with others, you may wish to compare your experiences before you make notes and close down (as indicated on page 139).

Eat a hearty meal after this particular journey – stamping your feet on *terra firma* is also a good antidote to any residual dreaminess! Over the next month, revisit the notes you made following your visualization and see what lessons you can take from your journey to the farthest shore.

Ensure that you anchor yourself on your return from the Samhain journey.

Imbolc reawakening

Imbolc witnesses the first signs of returning life after the darker days of the year. It is a time to sow seeds for new projects and renew our commitment to the principles we hold dear. This visualization helps emerge from the deep womb of winter, the darker days when our spiritual attention is turned inwards, into the light of the coming season when our attention will be turned outwards. Then we will work towards manifesting the ideas and potential we have discovered in the dark within ourselves.

This path-working acts as a catalyst to effect changes from within; at Imbolc we begin to move from concept or potential, to manifestation. Parts of this guided journey will require physical movement, so you will need to ensure adequate floor space, and some pillows or cushions to support your changing resting positions.

Imbolc is a time of emergence.

the
sacred
circle

The circle

I am a circle within a circle
With no beginning and never ending.

(POPULAR PAGAN CHANT)

The circle represents a universal and spiritually relevant paradox – a shape without beginning and without end. It visually describes eternity, the mysterious cycles of existence and the often uncanny circularity of our own lives.

Our ancient ancestors recognized the sacred significance of this shape and laid out many of their monuments in circle-form. Around Europe, for example, are the scattered remains of wooden and stone circles, aligned with specific stellar or solar rises and settings, many of which contain inner circles.

Many commentators have noted the yonic symbolism attached to such formations – that the circle represents that sacred place in the body from which women push life into the world. The fact that there are circles within circles seems to confirm the mystical association between the physical act of giving birth and the mystery of regeneration.

In Wicca, we do most of our ritual and spell-work within a circle, cast by a witch in order to define the boundaries of

The circle symbolizes the miraculous
cycle of existence.

the same, all circles are the one great circle of being, but every circle is different. We do not ever come out of the circle exactly the same person who goes in; it is like the saying that one can never cross the same river twice. By definition, the river changes because time passes, and the same is true of the circle. Within this progression of changes, the circle can be seen as a simple expression of the spiral – symbol of the eternal flux of all time-space-matter.

MAGNIFYING OUR EXPERIENCE

There is an additional and important reason why each circle is different; it is the space of transformation. If the circle is different each time, it is also true that whatever we take with us becomes altered in some way as a result of stepping

into it. Some witches notice early on that there is a sort of 'magnifying' effect at work within sacred space; this is a natural consequence of the intensity of what we experience there, and ensues from close contact with the realm of Spirit. What we carry with us to the circle grows in our consciousness to the point where we can see it

The spiral expresses the eternal journey of time-space-matter.

properly, occasionally becoming so big that we have to deal with it. This can be anything from a strength that we are failing to recognize and develop, to a bad habit that needs to be dealt with.

What we deal out to others within the circle, as in life, is what is returned to us; it is what we become. In the circle, this effect is amplified manifold.

TIME LAPSE

You may notice when you begin circle-work that there is a slight discrepancy in time perception between the world of consensual reality and the space between the worlds. Many witches notice that occasionally what seems to be no more than an hour in the circle is three hours or more outside of it. The most common experience seems to be the rapidity with which time passes in circle-space. It is not unknown, however, for the reverse to be experienced, especially when deep meditation work is being undertaken. On such occasions, celebrants may leave the circle feeling as though they have been away for hours, and find that only 45 minutes has passed. In tales of the Celtic Otherworld, human visitors to the world of Faery invariably experience a sense of time-disorientation; what passes for a day in the realm of Faery is found to be a year in the mortal realm, and seven years becomes seven hundred. It is tempting to speculate on the origins of these peculiar time-lapses, and whether the tales have absorbed aspects of tribal shamanic practice, where those who walk between the worlds experience time-changes.

The shape of the circle also describes the progression of our planet around the Sun. The circle is always cast *deosil* (pronounced day-sill) or 'sunwise' – clockwise. Traditionally, when building magical and ritual energy, celebrants try to ensure that they move deosil while in the circle to keep the energy moving in the right direction. Sometimes participants will move *widdershins* or anti-sunwise – anti-clockwise, when a banishing ritual is being enacted. When you become familiar with the energies that you work with as a witch, you will be able to decide what works best once you are within sacred space. However, the circle is almost universally cast deosil in Wicca.

Our ancestors left clues to their spiritual beliefs on the landscape.

Altars and sacred spaces

The classic definition of an altar is a place upon which sacrifices or gifts are offered to deities; if a physical description accompanies this definition, it suggests that an altar is a 'raised' structure or a 'high place'. Although this is a narrow idea of what an altar is, it does convey the notion that it holds things that are sacred and special, and may be a space in which gifts or offerings are left. In Wicca, our deities do not demand sacrifice; this much is clear in the Mother Charge – the words of the Goddess to the people, usually spoken in the circle by one of the participants (see pages 232–33). However, we do use altars in Wicca for several functions.

Altars come in many shapes and forms. They can be as simple as a flat rock placed in a shaded corner of a garden or woodland or as elaborate as an indoor permanent table decorated with embroidered cloths, canopied and covered in candles, statues or other sacred imagery. They might be temporary – for example, an altar set up for the duration of a circle and then dismantled. An altar can be a corner shelf in an apartment or a marble table on a hillside, but what really matters is the intent with which it is used. Its sacred purpose is what makes it an altar.

Incense is often used to consecrate sacred space.

SACRED CIRCLE ALTARS

An altar provides a focal point for sacred and magical activity within the circle. Traditionally set up in the north, but sometimes placed at the centre, the place of Spirit, the altar holds the tools and ingredients of ritual and may hold wands, *athames* (witches' knives), chalices, pentacles, initiation cords (see pages 200–01 and 226–29), bowls of salt and water, herbs, candles, crystals, mortar and pestle, or depictions of the

Altars provide a focus for spell-work and spiritual development.

deities. It also provides a practical working surface upon which to mix herbs, anoint candles, 'exorcise' water and bless salt (see pages 198–99). The ingredients for spells, once carried out, sometimes rest here until the end of the circle. When tools, spells or items need blessing or consecrating for a sacred purpose, they are brought to the altar – a place where things are made sacred, not just a place where sacred things are housed.

OUTSIDE ALTARS

Outside of the circle, altars serve many different purposes. In my garden, the big flat stone surrounded by many other rounder stones, planted around with rock roses and rosemary, is an altar to the Goddess. I have to sit on the ground to work on it, which brings me physically down to Earth. I use it as a focal point when I want to talk to the Goddess or a particular goddess, and I can burn

Altars can be placed indoors or outside.

incense and leave flowers or stones on it as offerings to her. In my home, the mantelpiece above the main hearth is an altar which variously houses offerings to particular goddesses, the physical ingredients for ongoing spell-work, candles and little offerings – feathers, flowers, cards, which honour the Goddess within. I have friends who have built altars that resemble shrines, out of stones and rocks and woven copper wire – these are focal points for meditation and visual journeys, spell-work, gifts to the Goddess, and a place to light candles to remember the dead.

Witches are also prepared, when need outweighs the principle of timing, to forego tradition. The guiding principle, as ever, is to 'Harm None' and if in order to stop or prevent harm we need to act quickly, then need, rather than convention and tradition, will direct our decisions.

Witches generally place the Moon phase above other considerations — except in urgent need.

Correspondences

The Five Elements Table

	Air	Fire
Spells	Communication, swiftness, exams, legal, knowledge and learning, conveyancing, travel	Defence, willpower, courage, inspiration
Herbs and plants	Lavender, eucalyptus, comfrey, wormwood, lilac	Rosemary, rue, dandelion, saffron, nettles, St. John's wort (*Hypericum*)
Trees	Birch, ash	Oak, rowan
Incenses and oils	Benzoin, sandalwood, lavender	Cinnamon, frankincense, vanilla, juniper
Astrological sign	Aquarius, Gemini, Libra	Aries, Leo, Sagittarius
Day of week	Wednesday	Tuesday, Thursday
Planet(s)	Mercury	Sun, Mars
Colour	Yellow	Red
Metal	Mercury (quicksilver)	Tin
Symbol	Upward pointing triangle traversed, feather, incense	Upward pointing triangle, flame, blade, salamanders
Magical tool	Wand	Athame
Animal totems	All birds	Salamander, big cats
Body parts	Lungs, head	Heart
Direction	East	South

THE ELEMENTS

The table below is a working guide to commonly recognized correspondences.

Water	Earth	Spirit
Love, healing, dream-work, women's cycles, childbirth, emotional issues	Manifestation, material wealth, shelter, fertility, growth	Initiation, transition, transformation, spiritual growth and knowledge
Poppy, rose, myrtle, violet, valerian, lovage, chamomile, geranium, hyacinth	Patchouli, sage, mandrake, woodbine, horehound, pennyroyal	Gentian, lotus, belladonna*, henbane* (*poisonous)
Willow, apple	Cypress, pine	Elder, yew
Myrrh, rose absolute, orris root	Patchouli, pine resin, white sage, mandrake root	Nag champa, copal, dittany of Crete
Pisces, Cancer, Scorpio	Taurus, Virgo, Capricorn	
Monday, Friday	Saturday	Sunday
Moon, Venus, Neptune	Gaia, Saturn, Pluto	Uranus
Blue	Green	Purple, white
Silver, copper	Iron, lead	Gold
Downward pointing triangle, cauldron, glass, mirror	Downward pointing triangle traversed, pentacle, wood, metal, stone, crystals, dragon	Upward pointing pentagram, terminated clear quartz, web, thread
Chalice	Pentacle	Cords
Fish, water-based mammals	Hare, wolf, bear, serpent	Spider
Womb, kidneys, bladder, liver	Bowels, spine	
West	North	Centre

PLANETARY HOURS

The table below is based on time divisions between sunset and sunrise. This may differ in your locality according to the time of year, so to pinpoint the 'hour' dedicated to the appropriate planet for a spell or ritual, calculate the number of minutes between sunset and sunrise, divide by 12 and number each unit one to 12. The planetary 'hour' that corresponds to your needs indicates what time you need to conduct your work.

Note that the following column is a rough guide — more comprehensive systems have a rolling matrix that differs according to the days of the week. For simplicity's sake, however, the following offers an outline based on numerological and planetary correspondence.

Sample calculation

For example, you wish to cast a spell to help a friend who is having trouble concentrating on her studies.

- The best planet to work with is Mercury.
- Your local times are sunset 9.30pm, sunrise 4.30am.
- The number of minutes between sunset and sunrise is 420, divided by 12 = 35 minutes.
- The first division of time after sunset ruled by Mercury is the third 'hour': 3 x 35 minutes = 105 minutes, 9.30 pm + 105 minutes = 11.15 pm.

pLaнeтaRy hоuRs тaвLe

Planet	Hour
Sun	I
Moon	2
Mercury	3
Jupiter	4
Mars	5
Venus	6
Neptune	7
Pluto	8
Mercury	9
Jupiter	10
Uranus	11
Earth	12

MOON SIGNS

It is now possible to download a reliable ephemeris, a table of predictions of planetary movements, from the Web, or in the appendices of good astrological guides. This will indicate when the Moon moves through different astrological signs and you will need to consult an ephemeris if you decide to work with the traditional correspondences outlined below. These indicate the best Moon-signs for different types of spell and are intended as an indicative guide, which you can add to as you progress in the Craft.

MOON SIGNS TABLE

Type of spell	Aries	Taurus	Gemini	Cancer	Leo	Virgo	Libra	Scorpio	Sagittarius	Capricorn	Aquarius	Pisces
Love/ relationships			•	•			•				•	•
Healing/emotions			•	•			•	•			•	•
Wealth/increase		•			•	•			•	•		
Employment/ commerce			•			•			•	•	•	
Banishing/binding	•			•		•		•				
Protection	•	•			•				•			
Fertility	•	•				•		•		•		•

DAYS OF THE WEEK

The following table, based on traditional Wiccan correspondences, can be extended as your studies in the Craft develop.

Days of the Week Table

	Monday	Tuesday	Wednesday
Planet	Moon	Mars	Mercury
Colours	Silver, pewter, white, grey	Red	Yellow
Deity	Selene, Nephtys, Artemis, Isis	Mars/Ares Tiew, Oya, Kali	Mercury/Hermes, Athene, Sarasvarti, Woden
Associations	Fertility, increase, dream-work	Defence, protection, inspiration, defeating obstacles, courage, sex, dance	Communication, learning, study, exams and tests, legal issues, travel, ideas, memory, science
Metal	Silver	Iron	Mercury
Symbolic object	Cauldron	Arrow	Staff

Thursday	Friday	Saturday	Sunday
Jupiter	Venus	Saturn	Sun
Purple, dark blue	Green	Black or brown	Gold
Thor, Jove/Jupiter, Rhiannon, Juno, Laxmi	Venus/Aphrodite, Angus, Parvarti	Hecate, Nemesis, Saturn	Brighid, Apollo, Lugh, Belissama
Generosity, natural justice, expansion, property, wills, family matters	Love, affection, friendships, partnership, allurement, sexuality, beauty, art	Boundaries, binding, exorcism, discipline, reduction, protection, deflection	Health, happiness, contentment, music, poetry
Tin	Copper	Lead	Gold
Drum	Rose, star symbol	Chain, cords	Disc

finding a circle name

The guided visualization outlined on pages 148–51 will help you identify a circle name. The following methods should be combined with this.

METHOD 1: NUMEROLOGY

Add together the numbers in your name in order to find your nominal number using the letters of the name by which you are known, and the numbers in your birth-date, as set out in the example below.

1	2	3	4	5	6	7	8	9
A	B	C	D	E	F	G	H	I
J	K	L	M	N	O	P	Q	R
S	T	U	V	W	X	Y	Z	

JOAN SMITH (born 25 October 1970)

J O A N S M I T H 2 5 1 0 1 9 7 0
$1 + 6 + 1 + 5 + 1 + 4 + 9 + 2 + 8 + 2 + 5 + 1 + 0 + 1 + 9 + 7 + 0 = 62$
$6 + 2 = 8$

Your new name should match this number when calculated in the same way. Joan Smith, for example, has discovered an affinity with the Goddess Andraste.

A N D R A S T E
$1 + 5 + 4 + 9 + 1 + 1 + 2 + 5 = 28$
$2 + 8 = 10$
$1 + 0 = 1$

If you are considering initiation with a group of people you work with and trust, do check whether they consider initiation to be 'into the Craft' or 'into the group', in case you are working at cross purposes. Many groups consider initiation into the Craft by their group to be an implicit acceptance and welcome into the group, but some do not and it is best to check how the other people you are working with actually see it.

Group-workings can amplify the energy raised for spell-work.

Initiation ceremony

The exact outline of an initiation ceremony differs between traditions, groups and individuals. However, some key elements are common to all initiation ceremonies and to this end it is possible to describe one here. There are some elements of initiation that cannot be outlined publicly, however, not because they cannot be revealed on pain of death or curse, nor because they are somehow morally 'suspect', but because there are some aspects of initiation that need to be kept aside for the occasion.

Although on the whole one should know in advance exactly what to expect of a ritual, there is an exception in one's own initiation. It may be, for example, that the exact question you are posed as you enter the circle (see page 228) is not known to you beforehand. Working out the answer in advance does not promote the same sense of immediacy produced by this 'surprise' element, and neither does it allow you to become emotionally and intellectually vulnerable before the Goddess in the way that you need to be. If you are working with sensible and kind people, there is nothing to fear from the odd surprise element being included in your initiation.

I should stress, however, that this trust should be given only to people whom you know and trust, and with whom you have worked for some time; the year and a day rule is good guidance here. Sexual activity is generally not a part of initiation until third degree in the Alexandrian tradition, and even then it is generally between a committed couple entering initiation together, or done 'in token'; the 'Sacred Marriage' is enacted symbolically with a chalice and athame, and not between persons. If you find anyone trying to convince you that initiation involves sex with them, steer clear and alert sensible people you can trust within the Wiccan community. Somebody who so disregards the meaning of Wicca cannot possibly have the sort of knowledge and spirit you need to guide you through initiation.

With all group initiations, the circle is cast and the elements are welcomed before the initiate is conducted to the circle. It is usual for initiations to be carried out 'sky-clad', or naked. This symbolizes your willingness to stand before the Goddess as you came into the world, without pretention or trappings, and is in imitation of the journey of the Goddess to the Underworld, where she gained knowledge of the mysteries of death. The initiate is blindfolded and may be

We enter the Craft in love and in trust.

loosely 'bound' with cords of their 'measure' (their exact height, head circumference, and distance around their heart) from one ankle to the wrists. He or she is led to a 'gateway' cut in the circle where a priest or priestess stands at the threshold to ask for the passwords and issue a challenge. The passwords are simply 'perfect love and perfect trust'. The challenge will be a posed question, however, and it is rare for an initiate to be told what this is beforehand.

In Wicca, the initiator kneels before the initiate.

What is very important, however, is that your coven should be able to trust you with confidential issues that concern the group. This means not revealing anything about coven-work to those outside, including naming those who belong to your group. Although things are getting better for pagans and witches in some parts of the world, witches are not always happy with others knowing their business. No one should consider themselves in a position to judge whether another witch would like you to reveal their religion or practices to others without their express permission. Keeping coven business quiet is part of discretion and knowing when to stay silent. Apart from anything else, running around boasting, even to other witches, what your coven did last week is likely to dissipate the power of whatever you managed to put together, as well as seriously annoy your co-coveners!

Covens are about consensual membership and that consent extends beyond the initial decision to join. You can leave at any time you wish, but you are bound by an expectation of discretion and confidentiality in the same way as you are when you are a member. The exception, obviously, is where you have serious concerns about some of their practices from an ethical view, in which case speak to a trustworthy and respected member of the Wiccan community for advice. It was once the custom for a coven to retain the 'measures' of a witch at initiation in order to ensure their silence. This dates back to the fearful times when betrayal could mean imprisonment or even torture and death to others. Because the measure is so intimately bound up with the witch's spirit, no witch would want to wrongfoot someone who possessed something that could be used against them magically. Nowadays covens give the measure back to the initiate and usually add the words: 'You are free to leave if your heart leads you.' Leave a coven if you feel that it is time to do so with a good heart and on good terms. You are entitled to do so without reproach.

Coven cooking

It is important to eat something after circles even if it is just the sip of juice and bite of bread passed around when it is time for 'cakes and ale'. But if your group is lucky enough to have kitchen facilities or a place to set up some food for afterwards, a communal post-circle meal can be very sociable! You can develop your own repertoire by researching which foodstuffs are associated with particular festivals, but the following recipes will get you started. The stew is good for cooking in a large pot over an open fire if you are on a camp-out together.

mooncakes

Makes up to 24 cookies

Ingredients

- 125 g (4 oz) soya margarine
- 50–75 g (2–3 oz) Demerara sugar
- 3 drops pure vanilla essence
- 125 g (4 oz) plain uncooked oatmeal
- 125 g (4 oz) wholemeal flour
- a little soya milk to moisten

Method

1 Mix the margarine to a smooth paste, adding the sugar and vanilla.

2 Blend in the oats and add the flour gradually, moistening slightly with soya milk to make a stiff dough.

3 Flour the work surface and rolling-pin, then roll out the dough to a thickness of approximately 5 mm (¼ in).

4 Using a crescent-shaped cookie cutter, cut out 24 cookies; place on a greased and floured tin, then cook in a preheated oven at 180°C (350°F), Gas Mark 4 until firm and golden, 12–15 minutes.

5 Cool completely before storing.

CIRCLe STEW

To satisfy very hungry coveners, serve this stew with couscous, rice or large chunks of wholemeal bread.

Serves up to 13

Ingredients

- 30 ml (2 tablespoons) olive oil
- 10 large garlic cloves, finely chopped
- 5 large onions, finely chopped
- 10 cinnamon sticks
- 1 teaspoon medium chilli powder
- 4 heaped teaspoons turmeric
- 8 large carrots, chopped
- 8 large parsnips, sliced
- 8 large potatoes, chopped into eight pieces each
- 2.7 kilos (6 lbs) tomatoes, chopped
- 3 heaped tablespoons tomato purée
- 2.1 litres (3½ pints) stock made with vegan stock cubes
- 1 level teaspoon low-sodium salt
- 8 large courgettes/zucchini, thickly sliced
- 675 g (1½ lbs) field mushrooms, chopped

Method

1 Heat the oil in a heavy-bottomed casserole, then gently soften the garlic and onion and add the spices.

2 When the onions are translucent, add the chopped carrots, parsnips and potatoes, stirring to ensure that they do not stick to the pan.

3 Add the tomatoes, tomato purée, stock and salt.

4 Bring to the boil, cover and simmer for 20 minutes or until the carrots are cooked.

5 Add the courgettes and mushrooms and continue to cook for another 10 minutes.

Working with fire

Candles should always burn down under supervision.

Fire is used in group circle-work in the form of candles that we light to honour the elements, the candles and lamps that grace our altars and those we use generally to light the ritual space. We also use incense sticks and cones, or charcoal discs on which to scatter blended loose incense. It is important, therefore, to ensure that coveners are safety-conscious.

It is a good idea to keep a fire blanket and a hand-held extinguisher in the ritual room. It is rare that such measures are needed, but it is better to be prepared than to risk dangerous accidents. If your coven works indoors, you should all agree on actions to take in the case of an emergency. This should include safe evacuation of everyone in the building and knowing the best exit points. If doors are locked during a ritual, ensure that everyone knows where the keys are. If you wear robes for ritual, make sure that these are not highly flammable, and watch out for sleeves and hems near candle-flames.

Much spell-work involves the use of candles. One method of using fire in spell-work is to anoint a candle with consecrated oil from bottom to top, top to bottom, then bottom to half way up. While doing so, you should think about the intent of your spell. When the candle is lit, it melts away the wax, releasing into the great web all the energy and intent that you have placed in the candle.

Another method for using fire as part of spell-work is to have a 'balefire', a sacred fire. If you are working outside you may choose to burn natural materials and to dig a fire pit, keeping a bucket of sand or water near by for safety.

- Heatproof mat
- Flower bulb, compost and pot

Casting the spell

1 Light the candle, saying: 'Old One, Wise One, Slow but sure One, Guide my spell and be it done.'

2 Hold up hair or signature, saying: 'I name thee [name]'s power.' Then wrap it in the paper and fold three times.

3 Place Epsom salts and alcohol in the fireproof dish (which you have placed on the heatproof mat) and light. Holding the folded paper say: 'As this Moon shrinks to bone, this spell shall burn your power down.' Throw the paper into the flame.

4 Hold the bulb before the flame saying: 'Out of the ashes I name thee [quality you wish the subject to learn].' Plant the bulb in the compost, adding the ashes to the compost when cooled.

5 Give the plant to be tended to the one who requested your spell.

Raising energy for spell-work

There are a number of ways to raise energy during spell-work, depending on whether one works alone or with others, one's mobility, the type of spell or simply the preferences of the person putting the spell together. The energy you put into a spell actually begins in the planning stages, at the very start when you are questioning the supplicant – or yourself – to find out what is really needed. There is also the energy of the concentration we lend to a spell while we are

gathering and preparing ingredients, and during the course of the spell as we imbue a symbol with our intent by our focused attention. However, there are specific activities employed expressly within circle-work to raise the energy in order to send a spell out into the ether.

While visualization and concentration produce their own energy forms, they are more generally applied in spell-work to focus on and imbue with our intent the symbols we use to represent what we wish to happen. The same can be said for the activities we engage in to bring the ingredients and form of the spell together prior to casting it. However, there are other kinetic, physical means by which we work to raise energy, including chanting and voice-work, anointing, drumming, dancing and lovemaking. There is more on sex magic on pages 274–75, which will explain the circumstances under which this method of raising energy is used and dispel some of the myths surrounding it.

The theory behind the physical means of raising energy is very simple – all existence in the Universe can be expressed as energy and movement produces and releases energy. Kinetic means of raising and releasing energy in a magically controlled environment serves to empower the spell and to propel it outwards onto the web. In groups, dance and chant serve to bond people to the purpose of the spell-work and act as a way of blending the energies of the participants. It opens the doorway to the deeper self, so that we can communicate outside of spoken or written language and move beyond the symbolic. This provides us with the means to move into an altered state, which better enables us to walk between the worlds.

Raising energy to empower a spell is basic to all spell-work.

Preparation through chakra work

Within our bodies are certain energy points. This has been common knowledge in different parts of the world for millennia, and some healing systems are based on the intricate knowledge of the way these energy points are joined together. In magical work, we open certain energy points in order to become more aware of the natural threads of the great web that are within and around us, and to enable us to conduct that energy to where it may do good. In the West, we have always been aware that we can hold, focus and direct energy through certain energy points on our bodies, even if we have not had a name for them. Since the increased interest in yoga and in Eastern religions, we have become familiar with the term 'chakra', and this is how we now describe these seven energy points.

Guidelines for opening the chakras are found on page 139 in the advice pertaining to preparation for visualization. This preparation is exactly the same for spell-work and ritual-work as it is for visualization; it involves us consciously enlivening and opening those energy points that help us direct and be a conduit for the energies within and around us. If you work with a group you may find that more experienced members have a moment's silence and concentration, and arrive at preparation much more quickly than is implied in these instructions. With practice and repetition the energy points are quicker to respond, and it is possible to enter very quickly into an altered state of consciousness.

Some groups prefer to run through the exercise of opening chakras or tapping into Earth/Sky energy and linking it in a loop through the body by having one member guide the whole group through the process. This works equally well. When some members become very experienced and sensitive to changes in energy levels, it is possible to reduce the time spent on this exercise because members will attain a suitably prepared level of consciousness in a very short time. There is no particular virtue in speed – and if you need to take your time this does not make you less powerful or an inferior witch – the point is to reach an appropriate state of preparedness, not run a race!

Crown chakra

Brow chakra

Throat chakra

Heart chakra

Solar plexus chakra

Sacral chakra

Base chakra

The energy points of the body.

Chanting to raise energy

Chanting is a traditional way of raising power.

Chanting is a good way to raise the type of energy needed to empower and send out a spell. The repetition, combined with the sounds produced, can be soporific, lulling the active, thinking mind into a state of momentary suspension, while the mysterious creative, 'right-brain' functions, which many magicians suspect is linked with psychic abilities, can come out to play. I have certainly experienced the 'lulling' effect, but cannot speak for which brain cells, if any, kicked into action as a result.

Different from chanting, voice-work, which aims to produce prolonged notes of specific frequency, teaches us that frequency can key into particular energies, which can be called into the circle and sent out again. There is a psychological and cultural element to this; minor keys, for example, are culturally linked with melancholy, mystery and the past and so may access energies within us that correlate with such associations. Elements of this are present in chant and, in combination with the principle of repetition and altered consciousness, this makes chant a particularly powerful tool.

Another function of chant is to help us focus; it helps if the chant is suitable for the proceedings. A good example of this would be using an upbeat, fast-tempo chant, the words of which relate to the element of Air for a communications spell. 'With my feathers I fly/As an arrow I fly/Straight to the arms of the Goddess I fly.' When working on a spell to bring about a transformation in your life, you might use the old Wiccan favourite: 'She changes everything She touches/And everything She touches changes.' There are many standards that are used in the pagan community, and you will hear many of these at camp-fires and at circles. However, some wonderful chants are available on CD and tape and over the internet on alternative and world music sites.

While chanting solo or with others can be a powerful way of raising energy, it can be wonderful combined with simple drumming patterns. However, if you use this method, you will need to ensure that the drumming does not drown out the voice. The drummer will need to be sensitive to the primacy of the chant.

Drumming, dance and visualization

Most methods of raising energy also serve to help participants make the transition from everyday consciousness to between-the-worlds consciousness. Drumming is an excellent example of this, and is often the chosen method for those who wish to enter into spiritual and developmental work in a drastically altered level of consciousness. There are theories about the links between the drum and our heartbeats, and psychology and musicology experiments have been carried out to map these connections. It seems that if we allow ourselves to 'enter' the drumbeat and concentrate on the rhythms, in some circumstances our own pulses alter to match it.

In circle-work, the link between drumbeat and pulse is used in much

Drumming aids a shift in consciousness to enable spell-work.

the same way as chant is deployed: to distract the left-hand brain functions; to tap into those psychological, physiological and cultural associations that are helpful in altering our state of consciousness; and to raise energy by calling it in and sending it out. Traditionally, drumming is for calling in, whether we are invoking an element, a deity or specific forms of energy. I have been to several festivals where drumming has been blamed for the torrential rains that seem to come out of nowhere to spoil an otherwise sunny day! However, I have also observed that drumming is good for 'sending' energy, too.

There are several different patterns of beat that help to raise energy and alter consciousness in a circle: waltz timing is popular because the three beats are associated with the triple Goddess; other rhythms seem to work just as well. Simplicity is of the essence, particularly if drumming is going to be combined with chants. Again, the best way to experience this is working in a circle where drumming is used or around a camp-fire. In addition, there are good DVDs, CDs and tapes of drumbeats used in Wicca, all available on alternative and world music internet sites.

The last form of raising energy for spell-work and ritual is dance – most often in covens this refers to simple rhythmic movement rather than complicated dance-steps. It is best for circles where people have full mobility, though I have participated in some pretty nifty formation wheelchair dances in the circle! The same principles apply as with chanting and drumming; dance is perhaps the most fully physical of these, and can be combined very effectively with both.

Kinetic movement such as dance is good for empowering ritual and spell-work.

Sex magic

Until relatively recently, it has been difficult to speak publicly about sex in a ritual context because of the sensationalist media inventions of orgies and the rather more damaging slanders concerning the abuse of minors. The care and protection of children is seen as a sacred undertaking in Wicca, so the wild and unfounded accusations against the community linked to allegations of so-called 'Satanic Abuse' in the 1980s particularly rankled. After the FBI and investigating commissions in other countries publicly concluded that fundamentalist Christian groups had deliberately orchestrated this 'blood libel', many witches chose to distance themselves publicly from any connection between ritual and sex. This is understandable as many Wiccan parents were concerned about the implications of social services taking an over-zealous interest in their child-raising abilities.

However, we are now moving into an era of greater tolerance and more public awareness of Wicca as a spiritual path as it comes of age. Just as Wicca has come to maturity, it follows that we should deal with sex in an adult manner. Needless to say, when I speak of sex and sexuality I am referring only to consenting adults; when I speak of 'sexual orientation' I am speaking of being heterosexual, gay or bisexual and some of the delicate nuances that dance between these definitions. Paedophilia – sexual interest in children – is not a sexual orientation; it is a dysfunction and if enacted is an act of violence.

Sexual energy is primal energy; it is a sacred form of energy which cultures believe brings humans closer to the divine. Between two freely consenting people, usually a committed couple who work together, sex in the circle raises energy that can be directed towards magical work. Provided that the act itself is in keeping with the rule 'harm none', it is as valid a method for engendering energy and sending it out as chanting, drumming or dance.

A controversy that has rumbled on for many years within the Craft is the issue of 'sexual polarity'. More accurately gender polarity, this principle is based on the assertion that all acts of magic must comprise a correct balance of 'masculine' and 'feminine' in order to make magic. This is unfounded: gay men, lesbians and bisexual men and women, men working together and women working together can empower a spell as effectively as a heterosexual male and female working together. If there is male and female in nature, there is also hermaphroditism and homosexuality.

Sex magic should be consensual and should be conducted with respect.

Directing and releasing energy

Directing and releasing energy takes place at various points in circle-work. Although part of the function of the circle's boundary is to contain energy until it is ready for release, this does not mean that it is raised throughout the circle only to be released when the circle is opened again. There are several points at which directing and releasing takes place.

The most obvious example of directing energy occurs when casting the circle in the first place. In this case, you draw energy through your body and direct it through the solar plexus, down the arms and through the athame blade, wand or finger to form a circle of energy. This is not, strictly speaking, a release of energy since the circle stays in place until it gently disperses and joins the Earth again or is drawn back through the person who originally cast it.

In a group there is sometimes a point when energy is released into the ether to go and do its work. An example of this can be found in healing work, where a circle of people holding hands first direct the

energy they are about to raise to a named person or persons. They say the name aloud, then visualize that person well and happy. The group raises energy by moving deosil in a dance, perhaps chanting. If a group is experienced in working together, there will be a point when everyone recognizes spontaneously that the energy has reached its optimum point. Some groups nominate a person to facilitate and judge when the energy is high enough and this person will signal when to release. Either way, when the time is ripe everyone raises their arms, hands still joined, and releases the energy skywards — sometimes with a shout or the last word of the chant to send it on its way. This does not break the circle, but it does release the energy raised for spell-work.

The two tools used most to direct energy in this way are the athame and the wand. The athame is most commonly used to cast circles, describe pentagrams and to direct energy when symbols are being 'named' as that which they represent. Wands can be used to cast circles, but are also commonly deployed when the element of Air is invoked to carry the spell swiftly onwards.

Many witches use an athame or wand with which to direct energy raised for circle-casting.

developing skills and knowledge

Developing your magical powers

Wicca is a path of learning; much of it experiential, some derived from research and study. Experience is most important, but acquiring basic information has its place.

There is a great difference, though, between information and practice, and the difference is knowledge. Knowledge is the deeper sense of realization that comes from direct experience of a truth. In Wicca, we can know what is true, but can only experience a truth for ourselves.

This is also true of 'the mysteries', a term you may come across in references to the Craft. Many people come to Wicca believing that because it is sometimes termed a mystery religion, certain secret information will be passed to them as they progress. The simple fact is that no one can teach or tell you the mysteries as these are realizations that reveal themselves as a result of your own spiritual experiences, through circle-work and direct contact with nature. You may find, when you try to share that knowledge, that you have trouble putting it into words, or that the

Learning about magic involves gaining new skills and developing your knowledge.

realization is so profound that it sounds simple and unimpressive when you try to express it. And perhaps that is as it should be.

You can develop your intuitive powers through visualization, dream-work and circle-work. It takes practice and sometimes comes in unexpected ways. Developing 'psychic' powers is not so much about predicting the winning numbers in the lottery as it is about enhancing your sensitivity towards random thoughts and learning how to decipher emotional changes within yourself. It may be as simple as having a sense of when the phone will ring or spotting coincidences and working out whether synchronicity is random or sometimes carries a particular meaning for you. This is part of being a patterner and a weaver of magic.

This section offers you a range of exercises to help you develop your abilities. It includes useful glossaries, outlines of Wiccan traditions and basic information on other relevant sources and methods of spiritual and magical growth. It is a good idea to start your own Book of Shadows now if you are working your way through this book gradually. This record of your own magical and spiritual development is a place to keep favourite magical recipes and results and can be added to as you progress in the Craft.

Meditation

Meditation is not all about transcendentalism or rising above the physical or daily reality of our existence – the separation of spirit and body is not an aspiration within Wiccan religion and practice. Meditation can take place in many different situations; some may include rhythmic movement such as dancing, digging a garden, knitting, spinning or weaving. Other stiller forms of meditation may include a focus of concentration such as gazing into a candle-flame. As one old hand once remarked to me after hearing a talk on chakra work and meditation: 'Meditation, eh? We used to call it looking into the fire.'

The objectives of meditation may differ; sometimes it is possible to meditate on a particular issue or symbol or question while carrying out repetitive physical activities. At other times it may be possible to practise being with a particular emotion or state of consciousness, initially by concentrating on an object or movement in the outside world, until we are still enough to be able to observe certain truths about ourselves and our dealings in the world.

Attaining a sense of stillness makes us more aware of energy changes within and around us.

Practising different forms of meditation will enhance and develop your skills in circle-work as well as your spiritual and magical development. Although one would hesitate to use the word 'discipline', practising the alteration of one's state of consciousness on a regular basis makes us more aware of those changes in energy that one encounters in the circle. See if you can perform a 'moving meditation' through rhythmic movement or when performing a repetitive task; is it easy to let your mind slip away from your surroundings? Or try focusing on an object and slow your breathing in order to enter a 'daydream' state of consciousness. Only experimentation will reveal what works for you.

Regular meditation also helps to enliven the spark of magic within by building our trust and understanding of our own intuitive powers. It also helps us build our inner strength as human beings, to discover our inner resources, our integrity and our beauty.

Regular meditation can help to broaden our spiritual and psychological vision.

Dreams and dream-work

Dreaming is such a mysterious activity that in spite of extensive scientific research, there is still no single theory on its purpose and function. Psychologists argue that dreams are symbolic of our inner desires. However, other evidence suggests that dreams help regulate our emotions, 'manage' and consolidate our memories, help us learn new mental skills and work through the tensions and stresses of the day. Dreaming also has spiritual significance.

The Major Arcana

0 The Fool	Beginnings, trust, foolishness, sagacity
1 Magus	Raw energy, preparation
2 High Priestess	Intuition, secret knowledge
3 Empress	Fertility, creativity, material matters, nurture
4 Emperor	Worldly power, responsibilities, command, oppression
5 Heirophant	Knowledge and wisdom, restriction, convention
6 Lovers	Relationships, passion, binding, obsession
7 Chariot	Movement, progression, delay, limitations
8 Strength	Control over the material, spiritual and physical alignment
9 Hermit	Enlightenment, wisdom, isolation
10 Wheel of Fortune	Cycles, rises and falls in status/wealth
11 Justice	Balance, cause and effect, righting wrongs
12 Hanged Man	Labour for gain, patience, suspension, stalemate
13 Death	Transformation, life cycles, resignation
14 Temperance	Life balance, thresholds, health, lifestyle, adjustment
15 Devil	Misconception, physicality, waste
16 Tower	Upheaval, disruption, irrevocable change, breakthrough
17 Star	Opportunities, lucky meetings, sharing wisdom
18 Moon	Intuition, female cycles, mental health issues, illusion
19 Sun	Health, success, happiness, generosity
20 Judgement	Understanding, resurrection, revival, bigotry, prejudice
21 World	Attainment, achievement, fulfilment

DIVINATION SPREADS

There are a number of standard divination spreads, for which guidance can be found in good Tarot books and on the Web. The best known is the Celtic Cross spread – an arrangement of ten cards, chosen at random and laid out and read in the following order with the labelled meanings ascribed to the card that turns up in that respective position. Another spread popular with Wiccans is the three-card spread for a direct answer to a specific problem or situation – three cards are chosen from the major arcana by the questioner and laid as below:

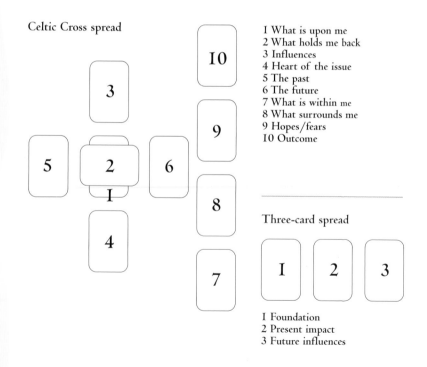

Celtic Cross spread

1 What is upon me
2 What holds me back
3 Influences
4 Heart of the issue
5 The past
6 The future
7 What is within me
8 What surrounds me
9 Hopes/fears
10 Outcome

Three-card spread

1 Foundation
2 Present impact
3 Future influences

Traditionally, a Tarot reader should be given her/his first set of cards, but many prefer to choose their own. Some people like to keep their cards wrapped in a black silk cloth or pouch and prohibit others, apart from questioners, from touching them. Witches tend to consecrate their decks in a circle, blessing the deck with purification incense (see page 342) before use.

MEDITATION

Witches also use Tarot cards for meditation. The 22 major arcana cards are a sequence of images, representing a cycle of the material, psychological and spiritually integrated progression of an individual. Given their significance, the major arcana provides opportunities for psychic storytelling and as a tool of focus for meditation. A good example of this would be the case of someone seeking to reconcile spirituality with the material and finding their own, innate median in this balance; an ideal card to focus on would be the Strength card. This card can be placed on an altar for in-circle meditation, or by the bedside as the first and last thing a person sees.

SPELL-WORK

The symbolism of the Tarot is particularly useful to witches in spell-work. When working a binding or banishing spell, for example, it is useful to have the Hermit card, which is associated with restrictive and disciplinarian Saturn, on the altar. This helps the spell-caster to focus on the particular form of energy they are summoning to witness and aid them in their endeavour. The power of a healing spell may be enhanced if the magician has the Temperance card present to help them concentrate on the nature of the work they are carrying out. Similarly, magical work for career success for a friend is benefited by the presence of the Star card, which symbolizes luck in opportunities arising.

Scrying

Scrying – which means 'to discern' – is the technique of focusing on a magical tool such as a mirror, a crystal ball or a flame in order to receive images and thoughts that reveal a truth or a message concerning a particular situation. In order to 'discern' the meaning of these, it is necessary to find the patterns present in whatever it is we have perceived – and we witches are great patterners.

The popular perception of scrying is that gazing into a magical crystal ball enables the 'reader' to physically see the future, rather like watching a video. Actually, there are very few people who experience this; the gift is peculiar to them and not the crystal ball. What actually happens when scrying differs between individuals. The theory about scrying is similar to that of chanting or dancing when preparing for magical or vision work. The craft occupies or distracts the left-hand side of the brain (which operates our thinking and rational faculties) in order that the right-hand side of the brain (equated with the random, the creative, the chaotic) is released from the

Using a crystal ball is one way of 'scrying'.

MERCURY

Mercury, planet of the messenger god Hermes, is associated with quicksilver ('quick' denoting 'alive'), also known as mercury.

SILVER AND GOLD

The first 'noble' metal in this table is silver, linked with the Moon, while the most noble of metals is gold, associated with the Sun, its life-giving properties and the symbol of spiritual attainment. The marriage of Sun and Moon is known as the 'Chemical Wedding' and Wiccans who honour both Goddess and God as aspects of the ultimate being perceive this as an expression of the balance needed in order to attain divinity.

Wicca tends to shy away from this type of hierarchical arrangement; we value the material world as being infused with Spirit rather than a graduation from 'base' to 'pure'. However, for Wiccans, alchemy captures the notion of spiritual attainment as coming out of the matter of the Universe; for us the idea that the secrets of the divine Universe are within and around us has a familiar ring.

The alchemical hierarchy of metals carries a specific meaning within Wicca.

Wiccan symbols

Like most religious paths, Wicca has its storehouse of favourite symbols. The attributes of some are multiple and subject to almost endless connotation and overlay. Some basic interpretations are generally agreed, however, and a brief glossary can be found below.

Witches often wear symbols and images on clothing or in jewellery designs. Occasionally, a symbol is carried or worn for a specific purpose, by way of invoking its power for protection or strength, for example. This is most often the case when we use them to decorate our magical tools, especially chalices, athames and wands or staffs. We also make good use of basic signatory symbols in magic and ritual by carving relevant signs into candles, writing them in ink or describing them in the air with our athames. Elemental and planetary symbols help to focus on the energies we invoke, and at the same time encapsulate their concentrated power.

Some symbols have been rediscovered from ancient sources – the spiral and the labyrinth – while those used for centuries for other purposes, such as mazes, have been reclaimed as sacred signs. Sometimes a path born in the West makes extensive use of symbolism that originated in the East; however as Wicca is an eclectic and diverse spirituality, it honours wisdom wherever it is found. Some witches like to keep to the symbols appropriate to their own particular traditions – but there is no orthodoxy dictating that this must be the case, and witches are more than happy to mix and match in the most respectful way.

THE PENTACLE/PENTAGRAM

One of the most commonly sported symbols in Wicca is the five-pointed star, the pentagram. If encircled it is a pentacle and signifies variously the circle of the Earth or the unified nature of the Universe. The five points pertain to the five sacred elements Air, Fire, Water, Earth and Spirit, and in this form it is

point of a household, or at the front and back doors, is an old way of protecting your home. They can also be woven into chaplets to be placed around the base of ritual candles or into circlets to be worn on the heads of participants.

Some witches like to make their own herbed oil by steeping concentrated amounts of herb in a good oil, such as grapeseed, leaving it for at least a week to absorb the scent and energy of the leaves and then pouring the oil from the jar or bottle onto a fresh set of leaves. This process should be repeated until the oil is thoroughly scented with the herbal perfume. Particularly successful herbs for this treatment are rosemary, basil, sage and thyme. This oil is considered extra-charged for magical use as the magician has already placed their energy into its preparation for sacred purposes. Both the energy and intent of the maker infuse the oil with the type of energy that is helpful to spell-work.

However you decide to use the following herbal, try to grow your own or pick them from the wild. Fresh herbs give out a different 'vibe' from dried (which can still be used at a pinch), and it is handy to have the fresh variety on hand. If you pick leaves and flowers from a plant, you should always ask the plant's permission – silently or aloud – and if it comes from the garden, bury a crumb of bread soaked with wine at its base as a 'thank you' to the Earth. If the glossary seems overloaded with

Fresh and dried herbs have different energies.

information, take heart from the fact that you are not expected to remember all of this at once and that this slice of knowledge can take a bunch of people a whole lifetime each to assemble.

FLORAL TYPES

Belladonna Also known as Deadly Nightshade, sacred to Lilith and Hecate, this is used in visionwork, banishings and bindings. Extremely poisonous and all precautions should be taken to prevent poisoning by contact.

Chamomile Used in a pillow to aid sleep and in incenses to aid meditation. Associated with success and money charms.

Honeysuckle symbolizes loyalty.

Carnation Sometimes known as 'clove flower', it is an energy-raiser and enhances the power of incense blends to which it is added. Also used in protection charms.

Cyclamen For love and protection; keeps nightmares at bay.

Geranium For use in love spells; good for countering anxiety and troubles of the mind.

Heliotrope Associated with solar deities, especially Apollo, heliotrope is used for prophecy and driving away negativity.

Lavender is one of the great 'Universal' herbs.

Honeysuckle May be used at handfastings to symbolize loyalty. Is used in prosperity spells, and to heighten female sexual energy if picked the day after Full Moon.

Hyacinth Dedicated to Aphrodite, hyacinth is a plant of love and its scent is reputed to relieve grief and keep nightmares at bay. Used in healing and love spells.

Jasmine Having Earth and Moon correspondences, jasmine is associated with women's cycles and sometimes used in spells to aid in problems with menstruation or conception. Used in love spells to attract a true and passionate lover, as well as in prosperity spells in line with its Earthy aspect.

Lavender A herb associated with Air and Mercury, excellent in communication spells and used in combination with other flowers in love spells. Good in healing spells for skin ailments and troubles of the mind. Excellent in dream pillows to induce sleep and help the sleeper remember their dreams.

Lilac The fresh flowers are used to induce clear memories and to enhance path-working and trance-work. Used in love and healing spells.

Marigold A solar plant, used in healing and success incense blends. Also used in love charms and sometimes threaded into a necklace to wish a bride good luck at handfastings. Used to bring the healing life force to healing spells.

Marigolds have solar associations.

Poppy A lunar plant used to induce prophetic dreams and bring healing rest. Associated with female cycles, it aids fertility and conception and helps regulate monthly courses.

Rose Sacred to Aphrodite, the rose enhances love-oils and incense blends. Associated with Water, it is also good for healing charms.

Soloman's Seal For protection, cleansing and decision-making.

Yarrow Wards off negativity, is associated with Air functions such as travel.

Roses are sacred to the goddess of love.

wands 201, 277
Water 31–2, 76–9, 84–5
    cleansing spaces 198–9
    correspondences 211
    scrying 300
    symbols 78, 315
wealth and weal spell 256–7
web 18–19, 30–2, 88–9, 244–5, 316
wheel, eight-spoked 317
white 320
Wicca
    colours 320–3
    cosmos 40–3
    covens 230–9
    deities 24–7, 100–1
    different paths 94–9
    elements 75–89
    gods and goddesses 103–31
    initiation 222–9
    magic 243–77
    philosophy and ethics 20–1
    rituals and ceremonies 365–81
    Sabbats 49–73
    sacred circles 185–217
    skills and knowledge 279–363
    spirituality 24–9
    symbols 314–19
    traditions 92–3
    visualization 133–83

what it is 16–19
Wiccan Rede 19, 22–3
wine 200
winter solstice 42, 50–1, 60–1
wisdom 16
Wiseman ceremony 372–3
Wise-woman 221
Witchcraft Act (1736) 94–5
witches, roles 220–1
    see also Wicca
Woden (Odin) 100, 128, 351
work, employment or promotion spell
        258–9

yellow 321
Yemana 84
Yule 50, 51, 52, 60–1

Zeus 115–16
zodiac 213, 290–1

Acknowledgements

Special Photography: © Octopus Publishing Group Limited/Russell Sadur

Other Photography: Alamy/Nigel Hicks 68-69; /Ronald Weir 38-39. **Bridgeman Art Library, London/New York**/www.bridgeman.co.uk/Bibliotheque Nationale, Paris, France 358; /Freja Seeking Her Husband, 1852 (oil on canvas), Blommer, Nils (1816–53)/Nationalmuseum, Stockholm, Sweden 125; /Lambeth Palace Library, London, UK 307; /Manchester Art Gallery, UK 363; /National Museum of Iceland, Reykjavik, Iceland 126; /Private collection, The Stapleton Collection 302; /Royal Library, Copenhagen, Denmark 129. **Collections**/Robert Pilgrim 360; /Brian Shuel 66. **Corbis UK Ltd**/58, 196; /Alinari Archives 106; /Bettmann 300; /Jim Craigmyle 178; /Gianni Dagli 117; /Macduff Everton 350-351; /Freelance Consulting Services Pty Ltd 190-191; /Greenhalf Photography 63; /Jason Hawkes 175; /Angelo Hornak 130; /Archivo Iconografico 311; /Mimmo Jodice 112; /Araldo de Luca 109; /David Muench 192; /Kevin Schafer 46-47; /Ted Spiegel 36; /Sandro Vannini 105; /Adam Woolfitt 189; /Roger Wood 118. **Mary Evans Picture Library** 122. **Getty Images** 21, 92-93, 168, 320, 369; /Adastra 209; /Richard Ashworth 100; /Ken Biggs 152; /Brand X Pictures 148-149; /Thomas Broad 22; /Comstock Images 30; /Nick Dolding 244; /Georgette Douwma 167; /Robert Everts 17; /Fischer 64; /Ken Gillham 367; /Peter Gridley 104; /A. Hansen 9; /Robert Harding 144; /Tom Murphy 142; /Fergus O'Brian 172; /Photodisc Green 241; /Planet Earth/Mike Coltman 164; /Jurgen Reisch 31; /David Sacks 34, 283; /Miquel S. Salmeron 19; /Tom Schierlitz 313; /Steve Taylor 353; /Adrian Weinbrecht 138; /Frank Whitney 67. **Octopus Publishing Group Limited** 16, 26, 33, 61, 70, 81, 82, 197, 250, 282, 284, 286, 290, 291, 292, 299, 324, 348; /Colin Bowling 328 top right, 329 bottom right, 330, 332, 336, 338; /Michael Boys 98-99, 326; /Nick Carman 72; /Jerry Harpur 51, 334; /Mike Hemsley 83, 204, 205, 217, 240, 345; /Neil Holmes 327; /Sandra Lane 331; /Sean Myers 32; Ian Parsons 65, 85 bottom, 143, 200, 294, 298, 323; /Peter Pugh-Cook 275; /Guy Ryecart 88; /Roger Stowell 325, 329 top left, 340, 341; /Mark Winwood 194; /George Wright 62, 328 bottom left, 333. **Nasa** 20, 208. **Rubberball** 4-5, 79.

With thanks to Mystics & Magic (www.mysticsandmagic.co.uk) for props borrowed on shoot.

Executive Editor Brenda Rosen   Designer Julie Francis
Managing Editor Clare Churly   Picture Library Manager Jennifer Veall
Executive Art Editor Sally Bond   Production Manager Louise Hall